# Fierce Delight

# Fierce Delight

## Poems of Early Motherhood

Emily Bright

North Star Press of St. Cloud
www.northstarpress.com
Since 1969

ISBN: 978-1-68201-160-7

North Star Press of St. Cloud Inc.
www.NorthStarPress.com

First Edition

Titles set in Cherry Blossom, Subtitles set in Amatic, Text Body set in Minion Pro.

"I wanted to explain
tiredness is expected
it is even appropriate
at the end of the day"

-Grace Paley, *For My Daughter*

For my family
with every line and verse.

# Poems

## And Suddenly I Was a Mother

## And Still I Was Myself

# I.

# And Suddenly I Was a Mother

# Pairs, and Soon a Threesome

Summer, and the trees are luscious. We stroll, eyes closed
to better smell the cedar. For once I am not forming words.

A bear cub lopes onto the road, like a dog, but heartier.
Carefree. Then ducks back toward Mama in the trees.

You trace my belly with your palms while baby spins
inside me. You can't tell yet, but she loves your touch.

Canoeing on the lake reveals half a dozen eagles. They mate for life,
you say. One surveys; its partner tucks against the pine.

In the ultrasound, we saw her face: ghost imprint of our dreams.
My heartbeat is her anchor. She was playing with her feet.

We wear bright colors while the sun lasts, take our dinners
in the breeze. Wonder sweet as this, you have to cup it in both hands.

## Preparing the Way

On the day my parents delivered me to college
with everything I thought I'd need: the guitar
I could barely play, the books (impressive and/or
loved), my very first computer with its promising
squat leaden monitor, my mother insisted
on making my bed.

I fussed over my dresser while she bent below
the top bunk, creasing hospital corners
as she'd done a hundred thousand times before.
My nurse-mother, whose hands taught us how
to make the patient comfortable; make the guest
feel welcome; keep the child clean and safe.

When I was still an act of her imagination,
still a swimming, pressing thing, she bought
one neutral yellow sheet, which she smoothed
and smoothed in expectation. Practice, perhaps,
for all the midnight sicknesses and accidents,
clean bedclothes tucked by rote in darkness.

Unfold the sheet. Center the crease. I was her helper
for a time, which meant I told her knock-knock jokes.
And, later, endless questions. And then I was
a teenager and edging toward something I could not
imagine but wanted desperately. And then we stood
sweltering in my tiny fourth-floor double,

while my mother tucked the patchwork quilt
she'd taught me how to sew. She knew that bed
might not be made again. She took her time.
I was urgent aimless energy, wanting parents to leave
before my roommate came. This was my remaking.
I wanted to spring fully formed, effortlessly cool.

My new blue towels matched my sheets. The pictures
on my desk all pointed back from where I'd come.
After they left, I sank down on my crisp-made bed
and stared out on the quad I hoped I would belong to,
trying to feel solid and solo and prepared,
glimpsing what I'm only now putting into words:

we don't get to know what we're preparing for,
not for ourselves, not for the children who hurtle
from our bodies onto their palm-sized feet.
We pack as best we can. We rise in the midnight hours
to give comfort, when we would rather sleep:
smoothing sheets, tucking covers,
building the habits of love.

# They Say You Forget the Pain

of labor, else why would we have
more children? (Smiles all around,
a little joke among mothers, deep
in the hazing ritual.)

And there you are, a new recruit.
Whale-sized. Quietly terrified.

There are libraries' worth of
details they won't tell you. Books with
color illustrations that, let's face it,
you don't really want to see.

There is prenatal exercise,
the class you drag yourself to weekly,
in which thin cheerful women
whose backs do not hurt daily
preach the power of squats and
kegels for a confident delivery.
Do you really want to practice,
to hold poses for one minute to
simulate contractions?

No,
you want a second dinner and
odd food combinations: strawberries
and pickles, say, or pretzel fudge. You want
shoes that shuck off without bending,
sleep with no one kicking you.
You get nightly workouts rolling over.
This, too, no one ever mentioned.

And after labor, what words are there,
really, to sing your foxhole hours,
the murderous muddled fantasies
about the epidural doc
who showed too late,
the pangs that de-articulate,
the blessed calm moments in-between
that grow fewer and shorter—
the narrow passage—
then, the strength
you yank from within you that thrusts
forth
life.

Nobody will tell you
that the thrill of recognition
when you first (be)hold your child
does not instantly erase
the struggle that came before.

# How We Fit Inside the Systems

You were born in a hospital three hours from home
	because rural America.
My husband spent the year
saving up his sick leave
	because no parental leave
	because that's how it goes.
And so he went back to work
stunned and waiting for your NICU release
while I stayed at the Ronald McDonald House
where volunteers brought home-cooked meals daily
	because kindness
but when I filled out the forms to stay there—
child's name, mother's name, father's name—
I wrote down my parents' names
and had to ask for a clean sheet
	because we were parents now
	because you.

# Preemie

How we scrub our hands and forearms with pink hospital soap
eagerly, determined to protect you from every unseen threat.

How we creep into that soft, dark room lined with incubators,
find you, first one on the left,
swaddled, nearly always sleeping
with a face so much like mine
my breath catches every time,

the IV in your peach-fuzz hair secured with a white-tape bow,
an "It's a Girl!" touch to match the rolling cast of duckies,
monkeys, smiling frogs, all soft fleece preemie jammies
with cavernous, rolled sleeves.
The nurses dress you every day.

How monstrous I feel by comparison.
How I measure, knowing later I will doubt
how small we can start out and thrive:
your body to my forearm
your face to the length of my finger
your impossible formed fingernails.

How suddenly our context shifts:
the water breaks six weeks too soon,
and there you are:
dark eyes wide,
tongue tasting air,

and now we're cheering every ounce you gain
while down the row of incubators
another set of parents learn the alphabet
of cardiology. Another mom delivers milk
she pumped for twins born less than two pounds each.
"They look like barbie dolls," the father whispers.

I am not grateful-by-comparison.
I am grateful, period. And tired.
And clinging to assurances that one day
like a light switch flipping, you will have the strength
to eat enough and grow enough
and then you can come home
to everything unknowable
that happens next.

# Savor

It is a regular bone of contention I pick with my husband.
Food deserves to be savored, I say, while he says our meals labor
on and on. He gulps and finishes, ready for what's next.

And then our daughter, fittingly, is slow to nurse her first
two months, always craning her head to look around, catnapping
at my breast. Ma petite gourmande—I spend so many hours
in that rocker. I tell my husband, soon he'll be outnumbered.

We parry our food weaknesses: his furtive double Whoppers,
my hidden stash of chocolate. We are, as we were raised eating:
his family, fueling on-the-go between adventures,
mine lingering at the table until each academic topic had been
thoroughly picked over. And now we've made, between us,
a squalling, blue-eyed mystery. I let my daughter linger, saying,

"This is what I've made for you. Milk my body formed
from fruit and stew and bread." She works her little jaw
so earnestly, while her eyes dart everywhere. Her feet
kicking, which is what she does when she is happy:
four months old, she kicks and smiles, and we both,
my husband and I, we both just eat it up.

# Rocking My Baby to Sleep

After she finally stops squirming, launching out against my ribs
in total confidence that I will hold her up,

After she lays her head upon my shoulder, then looks up
like a prairie dog to see what she might miss
(my dinner getting cold, my husband ready with our movie)

After she plants her thumb securely in her mouth and spreads
the other soft warm hand against the pulse of my neck,

After I run out of songs and stand just rocking quietly, watching
her eyelids in their slow blink toward sleep,

After all this, and before I lay her down, I remember, finally,
to let my body rest. I release my arms, my neck.
Let her body lower against my body.

She stirs and I breathe, recalling what I wish to be pressing into her.
Not my worry nor my rush, but something deep and simpler:

A full, sweet sleep; a happy waking. In the night-lit dim I hold her.
Let these hands be hands of blessing.

# Take This Moment, Too

There will come a time when you
cannot think past the children, when
Philosophic Thought is a slim volume
on the shelf, tucked back
behind the bottles, and you know
how it is to reach back there:
caps go rattling to the floor,
the baby thinks it's all a game.
And so you play. You grin and burble
through the mundane. Clothes
need matching. Dragons romp inside
the vacuum. You master other formulas
involving peas and squash. That degree?
It's folded somewhere.
You half-believe that when you find it,
you will recognize yourself.

# After Children

It never fails. The doorbell only rings when the baby's crying,
face painted with sweet potato, and whatever interrupted you
will not be worth the fuss of getting up. The delivery guy
already driving off, say, having dropped off something you don't need:
baby clothes in an outgoing size, sent from a distant relative.

Whoever promised an ordered life sold you a real whopper.
Who was it? Someone on TV, no doubt, someone with a make-up crew
and a full-time staff. Everything still matters, all the old desires and
concerns. You're you, re-centered, after children.

Now the baby does not want to eat. She wants to bury her face
in your shoulder and smear her cheeks semi-clean. You let her.
You would let her do almost anything (a fact you hope she won't
discover). Which is why, when the man you love (the man
you used to call nightly just to hear his voice, before you wed)
the man you now call Daddy finally comes home in the middle
of her bath, and she does her crazed squeal of recognition,
you understand that clean is relative. You hand off your soapy child
like a hot potato, not caring that he, too, must balance a new act;
you rush out into the fading winter sunlight for 10 minutes,
    unencumbered,
trying to remember when walks like this were normal, knowing
you didn't appreciate them nearly enough.

# One Hour Past Naptime

I wanted five minutes to finally sit;
she dunked her fingers right into my tea
and shrieked in her shock. (I had just poured it.)
She reached up her hands, for comfort, to me.
Part of me thought, as I leapt to my feet
and shushed, "My poor love, I've got you, don't cry,"
how precious to have a trust so complete.
(The rest of me kissed my poor "me-time" goodbye.)
I held her in one arm and grabbed for a tissue,
with one hand I wiped down all that was wet.
I kissed her fingers. That solved the issue.
She nuzzled her head down (at last!) on my chest.
I eyed my (cool) tea, but didn't dare rise.
"You just take a rest now. Isn't that nice?"
I kissed her soft hair. She fluttered her eyes.
Her breathing went gentle. I took my advice.

# In the Sunlight of this Morning

In the Tuvan language, spoken in dwindling numbers
somewhere deep in Russia,
there are verbs which tell us we go backward to our future,
forward to our past.
Once I bent my thoughts into their new direction,
I thought: yes. Isn't the past
what always spreads most clearly before us?
Yesterday's burnt steak, last night's
sleep-blurred argument, the lines so care-worn
we could speak them in the dark.

In the sunlight of this morning, our daughter
is discovering new planes of existence.
The table top, the toilet lid, the bathtub is
the rim of some new wonder, now
that she can pull herself to standing.
I stack toys for her to rediscover.
All day, she'll peer and reach. She'll trail me,
crawling room to room while I
try to accomplish tasks from my long list.
This is as far as I can see backward

into the day. Just behind my shoulder lies
everything else. We slept in anger,
apologized this morning over her spoon-feeding.
You left to run your meetings.
I lifted our daughter in the air and
helped her balance on her feet, still thinking
about dying languages, how across the globe
they try to tell us where to look and
what to build upon. We need as many words as possible
for what is precious.

Like the way we greeted each other in the
 sunlight of this morning, sheepish and
determined to try to listen better. Like the way
 our daughter squirms with frenzied joy
out of the arms that hold her each time one of us
 returns, proclaiming hoarsely "Dada,"
which is her word for both of us, and which,
 as I lean in to fit her precious body
to my body (the life our lives have made together)
 is enough to make me turn myself,
finally, to this moment: grateful for each homecoming,
 each offering of love.

# Dartmouth Scientists Discover High Levels of Arsenic in Rice

## 1. Negatives

"It was inevitable: the scent
of bitter almonds
always reminded him
of the fate of unrequited love."
I never finished Marquez's *Love
in the Time of Cholera*,
never got past this first line,
but still it dug deep into me.
Ever since, I've pictured arsenic
as the photo-negative of
that sweet nut. Something almost
good for you.

## 2. The Morning Before the Radio Report

I make the yum-yum face, spoon cereal
into my daughter's mouth. She opens
with a steady *mmm* that has not yet linked
to vowels. Mama, I say, mmaaa-mmaaa,
and she grins her two-toothed grin.
My mother predicts genius, as all grandmothers
do. I nod. I hope most days for normal (plus).
Most days, I hope she'll take a decent nap.
I spoon another baby mouthful, thinking
I'm helping her grow.

## 3. What Looks Familiar

"Time for your arsenic, dear," the old hag croons,
a bowl of poisoned oatmeal for the lover she never
liked. Another line that's dug-in-deep, this one from
Dylan Thomas. I still can see her shuffling,
smiling, spooning in her patient dose.
I've watched those murder mysteries enough
to know the signs: the patient, bedridden,
hair prematurely gray. Heart shutting down.
Oh. That again. I sit back,
shuffling through the candidates:
the fed-up maid, the jealous mother.
The victim changes diet and
presto! Problem solved. Except
his trust had leaked away. Except
he's feeling heavier. Those metals
built up month by month—
where do they go now?

## 4. Be Cautious, Say the Scientists.

All the food's "All Natural"
down my grocery aisle. My daughter gapes
at colored packages. She wants
to put them in her mouth. I patrol
the labels, sneering at the rump roast ("On Sale!"),
thinking there's always nature somewhere:
cows eating corn / cows eating all-natural
cows and penicillin / caged
chickens / rat feces in factories /

this is how the garden grows
at the FDA's safe [ ] levels.
[Some] arsenic has always
dwelt in soil.
So?
So shake Rice Krispies
in frustration, then put them in the cart.
Get angry / get paranoid / just give up
and go out to restaurants where
you don't have to know.

Here's a pretty package. Somebody in Corporate
laughs at my hypocrisy, saying
you don't complain of arsenic
when you wear U.S. cotton, you don't
complain about variety / abundance /
thanks to pesticides, you can cut out rice
entirely and still feed your family.
Choose the shiniest apple, my dear.
Now say thank you and go home.

Now my baby squawks for us to get a move-on.
It's dinner time; we're hungry. Her baby food's
all natural and sweetened with brown rice.
I'm railing. I am adamant. I will save her
from the dangers we discover one by one,
save her from the tired,
tiny part of me that says
we've made it
this far:
what can a little bit more hurt?

# Just Wait

Some moments I am already preparing myself to miss,
like the way she falls asleep with her hand upon my chest,
palm to heart, warm fingers as her breath slows and deepens.

It's the fears that cling like slugs—the suspicion that this lollipop
or that missed nap will lead, straight and slippery,
to an angry school principal calling, some years down the road.

My daughter can walk now. Her stance still wide and
stuttering, she wants to choose her own direction. I know,
I know what you would tell me, how this is a foretaste.

The parents who taunt "teenager" like an impending
penalty. They gaze at us across the grocery aisles, thoughts gauzed
with nostalgia. "Glory days," they whisper, invoking

their grown ones who are no longer mollified with Cheerios.
I do not wish to love my life in retrospect. And so,
I let her balance on my shoulders and spread her arms like wings

as we wait for the harried cell phone tech to call the next in line,
while around us, the bald man here a quarter-hour, the blue-haired
grandmother, the biker in his jacket, grin back unabashedly
as (not) only children do.

# Fierce Delight

In the pew
(came late, stuck
behind the pillar)
I'm flattened
once again
by the urge
to pray.
Most days
I can't get silent
enough, nor still.
I launch prayers
like arrows
while scrambling
the morning eggs.
Can I say this?
I don't feel
productive, praying,
unless I'm the one
who's speaking
which, of course,
is not the point.
But today,
the desire to be
immersed
and present
draws me like my
favorite song.
I toss aside
the laundry listing,
let the sermon

hum.
I'm here, I say.
I'm listening. But soon,
I'm thinking once again
how much I love
my child. I mean,
it would be sinful
if it weren't
a God-reflected thing—
this mother-love.
This fierce delight.
Trying to get back on track,
I catch
a wiggle of God,
a resonance
of Presence
which is enough,
which says

YES. DELIGHT.

And now I'm praying
with new hands
and spirit:

may every child
in the world
be delighted-in
and know it.

I sit, bathed in longing,
one point in a global
web repeating this un/

remarkable prayer
until it's time
to leave again,
to rise and greet
and go make lunch,
to live out
this delight
and not
be turned away.

# At Home

I have invented nothing new today.
I have not bled nor bargained.
I've baked no winning cakes.
I have not walked an hour to haul water,
nor gambled my last dollar.
The dogs I don't own are unfed.
I've spoken no unkindnesses, at least.
I've had no visionary dreams;
and if we've landed on the outer rings
of Saturn or witnessed another shooting,
I have not read reports.
I don't plan to remember how
I hung the laundry, nor stooped
to retrieve, repeatedly, the toys
that held my daughter's fascination
one minute at a time. Our morning
has pulsed steadily into afternoon.
I have not taken everything for granted:
how, after sifting flour, yeast, and water,
I lifted her small body to my hip
so we could watch the bread machine
mix the stuff to sustenance. The dough wobbled
and puffed its fine white breath into our faces.
I have not saved a life today, nor cost one.
Perhaps I should have offered my attention while
the dough rose silently and became our bread.

# Mother's Day

My second Mother's Day,
which I'd hoped might be a day-of-me,
began at 3 a.m. Your fever spiked
again. You woke us, glass-eyed,
whimpering. Radiating heat.
We debated, consulted books by harsh light.
You wanted only to be held, to crawl back
inside of me. Naked but for diaper.
I fought the urge to swaddle you.

At 4 a.m. on Mother's Day
I took you to the shower,
let the water, cool on my skin,
pound like ice on yours;
I held you for your own good
and dried you, squalling,
while your daddy hovered.
We sunk into the couch, your daddy
and I, bathrobed, hyped with stress,
fearing every complication we'd read.
Tired in our marrow bones.
I held you in your misery.

Somewhere before the dawn,
you snuggled in, and slept.
The hour became
no longer about you.
We lingered, your daddy and I,
sleep-smeared, speaking uninterrupted,
aware the sun
was rising of its own accord
beyond the pines.

Was it romantic, watching sun
leaven day together?
Not in that weary moment.
But by now you know how
love can rise like steam, like heat,
like oil from the stew.

# No One Ever Said We Couldn't.

It has been a year since my last poem.
I admit I've been all diaper changing, plodding
novel revision, jaded after teaching freshman
that a poem is more agile than the scraps
they've been exposed to. But it's April,
and the teacher asked me during yoga,
as a favor. Sure, I said from downward dog,
I'll talk to your fourth graders.

Now they look up from their desk clusters,
eager for a new face. I read a couple
of my favorites, give them goofy exercises.
They clamor to read what they have written,
double-spaced and loopy, some with runtogetherletters.
"The sea was black and grumbling,"
one girl writes. I praise her phrasing,
recalling how my *professeur* raved about
my poetic use of words in French—
I didn't know I couldn't, so I did.

I may have wrecked a month of 4th grade
grammar lessons. They're inventing verbs,
forgetting punctuation. I encourage them.
Worse, I mention e e cummings.
Let their teacher sort it out.

Now I am remembering so many things I love.
They illustrate while I recite *The Walrus*
*and the Carpenter.* "The sun was shining on the sea,
Shining with all its might...
And this was odd, because it was
The middle of the night." We revel in
what shouldn't be. They clap when I finish.
Ten year-olds with silly words, they need
no convincing. They love poems along with me,
for no one ever said they shouldn't.

# The 23rd Psalm,
## As Enacted by My Third-Grade Sunday School Class, Becomes a Harrowing Primetime Drama

The wolf is eight years old and eager.
He didn't volunteer for this gig
just to get fended off by some gentle
shepherd. Ditto for the sheep-snatchers,
twin sisters, who might or might not have
a cousin in the flock who deserves
some old-time retribution.
The sheep crawl behind me, bleating
and chomping their way through green-carpet pastures.
Unafraid, they scamper through the narrow
Valley of Chairs. We all know it can't go on
this way. At first wolf-launch
(yes, launch and wrestle) two sheep play dead
with flair, tongues lolling, feet in the air,
until I restore them body and soul
and tell them to get a move-on, please.
Cue the sheep-snatchers. The cousin turns
ninja, rising up miraculously on his two sheep-feet
to throw a roundhouse kick, which misses,
miraculously. No passive sufferers, they.
In this play, there are no drunken fathers,
no homeless winters, no dead pets. We beat a hasty
retreat, shepherd-me in rear guard, lifting
lost sheep bodily, as it sometimes goes
in real life, from the precipices
of Chair Valley, where they threw themselves
because don't we all want to be rescued?
Safe at last at home base, they collapse

in giggles and reach for apple slices,
wolves and sheep and snatchers all. We conclude
that everyone has their work cut out for them:
the Shepherd who does all that saving,
the sheep who can't tell where they're heading,
even (why not?) the wolves. God does not
get tired, I say, of the search-and-rescue.
Done with snack, they want to play it again.

# Still Life

She could not reach the counter
so we made muffins on the floor.

We greet the sky daily:
hi sky, boo sky, nice sky.
She is always thrilled to see it.

She woke & screamed an hour
for reasons that seemed good to her.

It's still possible I've ruined her
and just don't know it yet.

We watched the churning cement truck
birth a new foundation near our house:
her most enthralling morning yet.

Why do I answer each "how are you?"
with reports on how my child slept?

It's possible everyone else
is doing a better job at this.

She and the moon are fast friends.
Hi, Moon! Nice moon! she sings from her car seat,
ignoring our efforts to put her to sleep.

At unexpected turns, I see
the parts of me I love, reflected.

I'm almost sure she has the habit down,
but I still peek in to check her breathing.

# Miscarriage

## I.

The one that wakes us up from sleep.

The one we can't confirm.

The one we felt wiggle and shimmy
and then stop.

The one we have to un-tell friends and family.

The one that nearly kills us.

This is no inner circle, we women
who have missed / misplaced / miscarried:
such a fumbling term, as though
you'd set it down somewhere.

The loss remains internal. Nuclear.
A slow leak.

## II. Ectopic

"What clown operated on you?"
my doctor asks, critiquing his own handiwork:
a triangle of incisions across my abdomen.
A jagged "J" bulges from my belly button.

The explanation is simple: a zygote lodged
and multiplied, swelling my tube
"to the size of a bratwurst," then burst,
bleeding me from the inside.

I could have died screaming.
Women die this way each year, still. But me:
just three incisions, recovery dragging itself
across a month, a gnawing fear.
Next time, there is no back-up part.

I tell my doctor
I don't mind the scar.

# The Body Wants

The logic of the body
does not trouble to explain itself.
It is not satisfied with just one beautiful
healthy child. The body wants.
And the waiting, oh—
as though the clocks have slowed,
the constant scanning for
this twinge of nausea, this ache
within the breast.
Impossible to stop the arithmetic
that adds nine months
to everything, that hesitates
before buying that dress, that coat,
that might (please, God) not fit
next season. The body wants
with an ache primeval; every passing moon,
every waxing figure on the street
every car seat tucked in someone else's
shopping cart, even as hope trembles, wanes,
the body goes on wanting.

# Near-collision

The oncoming driver in the minivan becomes mother-wolf.
Her eyes devour. I slam my brakes. She bares claws and fangs
through her closed window as she speeds through the suburban
intersection. I know from her expression there are children
in the back, snug and buckled, preoccupied with snacks.
They don't suspect our near-collision, nor the violence
in their mother's stare that leaves me breathless. I am seventeen,
ensnared by homework and the prom, careful not to scratch
my mother's car. There is nothing in my whole life yet
for which I'd claw through wreckage. No one for whom
I would tear meat from bone: not in vengeance nor defense.
I can't tell you in that moment that I glimpsed my unborn
children and the feral love I'd bear for them. I can't tell you
I suspected my own mother's fierce protection, nor did I recall
the time my father charged faster than I'd ever seen to catch
my sister, mid-plummet, between the splintering tree branch
and the stream. No—I am seventeen: shaken and indignant, explaining
to my empty rearview mirror why I'm not a villain.
I drive home, haunted by the ancient and the future in her stare.

# Playing House

First and most important was how to get rid of the men.
Father's gone to war, we'd say, it's just us girls in charge.
Father's at work. Father's dead. No one wanted to play a boy.
I always wanted to be ten when choosing my pretend age,
until I grew to almost nine and ten became too real.
Then thirteen: grown-up age.
From the trunk we selected skirts and dresses, the hot pink
molting feather boa. It was always the 1800s, because
that's when adventures happened. We tried, one summer morning
to round out the family, cajoling the neighbor boy
'til he gave in. He stood there stupidly, refusing to dress up
or help save the village or take mother dancing, and soon
we all went back outside to chase fish in the stream.
Later, friends gone home, I went hunting in the shadowed
basement where we kept our Christmas boxes.
I killed the dragon, blinding it with my sparkly heart necklace.
When I told my neighbor of my daring conquest, he was busy
building, fitting all the pieces like the picture on the box.
Blue on green he stacked the castle wall or spaceship taller,
so I went back to "girl games," and kept the village safe.

# Jade

It is a most forgiving tree.
It wants so little: the dregs
of coffee, sun filtered through
a window, a yearly change of soil.
It grows without my asking,
uncomplaining, in the same old pot.

I mothered it, sporadically,
before I was a mother: wiped
its leaks from the sill, murmured
thoughts into its branches,
brought it ladybugs for play.
Worried when we went away.

But most times I left it
to twist branches as it wished against
the window glass, until it leaned
so hard toward sun it couldn't stand
alone. New pillowed waxy leaves
popped out without my counting them.

A plant is not a child, though
it loves in its own way. And when
I thought to limit all the things I had
to care for, when I left it, potted,
by the dumpster in the snow,
it did not necessarily start crying.

Though I swear I heard it.
I scooped it up and stroked
its smooth bark in apology.
Forgiving plant, I whispered: Please?
And set it back upon the sill.

# Haikus:
## Nature Hike with Toddler

On the nature trail
we explored a hundred yards
very thoroughly.

At first, I urged her—
we had a loop to finish.
But then I thought, why?

I trailed behind her,
bearing her pinecone treasures
She knew when one dropped.

Above, leaves chattered,
blushing, crinkling, yellowing
by their secret clocks.

She watched her first squirrel
climb and chirp. She learned its name.
I got to teach her.

# Meadow For a Memory

My husband and my daughter are strolling after dinner
through the lot behind our house. They investigate
the dirt piles. They gather rocks like endless treasure.
In a moment I will have to call her in for bed.
I cross my arms against the chill, try to memorize the scene:
the way they wobble over rutted ground, her head just high
enough to rest his hand upon, which he does reflexively,
stroking the wild blondish fuzz that he passed down to her.
I will erase the cars that whoosh past the border of the lot,
erase her napless afternoon, the looming bedtime hour
that might (or probably won't) go smoothly. I consider
giving them a meadow for this memory. Wouldn't flowers
be more scenic than lumber and a construction crane?
(Now they're pausing to examine grooves the trucks
have left behind.) They recite the story book we've read
three times today. I don't think I'll remember that,
if I have my way: just the indistinct and happy murmur
of their voices, the smoke of our pine campfire. Let them be,
five minutes more. Let the dirt puff over her yellow rain boots,
dusting her pajamas, which I had hoped to keep clean for bed.
Let every detail fade, save this: just a man and his little girl,
my two beloveds, ambling, while the sun lingers behind.

# II.

# And Still I Was Myself

# Googling My Name

I am young. Blonde or brunette.
I study business, family services, the law.
I died of ovarian cancer last January;
I had an unswerving sense of humor.
I teach math in Delaware,
high school French in West Virginia.
Here, I'm feeding apple juice to children.
I am British and American.
I won the Junior Olympics in track.
In Iowa, I am a champion baton twirler.
I star in a romance novel, a headstrong heroine
in frontier Montana who lands both man and claim.
(I look dramatic on the cover.)
I am track 5 on the Backfish album.
I'm "bent toward environmental activism."
I look familiar.
Here, I'm watering a garden.
Here I've entered Arizona Pride's Clogging Competition.
In Florida, (grade 3), I'm student of the month.
I died with so much peace and hope,
my dear friend wrote a book about my one resonant life.

# And Here's to Naiveté

We're on a string of arsons now he traced back to the mayor. It was insurance fraud, all hush-hush. "Guess I found out too much," he says, leaning across our little table. His Jack-and-coke's half gone. I am naïve enough to ask what happens next.

"My own editor wouldn't back me. I had to get out of town." He's taking in my details not-so-surreptitiously. New intern at his waning hometown paper. Legs crossed tight, short skirt, but still professional. Isn't this what they say to do? Ask questions if you want to learn?

His swagger's choking me. It'll take a month before I understand he didn't really want to see my writing.

He has a hunch about the gal who killed her baby. "She was hearing voices," he says conspiratorially. Two times he calls me beautiful. He says, "In my line of work, you've got to know where to look. You start to wish bad things would happen, just for the career, you know?"

Drink drained, I drop him off, too polite to rebuff his hug across the car. Ready to slap—I tell myself—if he cops a feel. But there is no gross invasion, just my squirming realization of the way things are sometimes, even now, and what am I going to do about it?

# The Important Parts

And now we've reached the point
  where I know many things about her,

save her name. I've met her autistic son,
  who follows her to work sometimes.

He needs someone to wipe him off,
  to dress and bathe him, at his age,

and he lets only his mama. How tired it
  makes her, how devoted. "I cry,"

she says "I'm tired, but my God is good."
  She tells me this in bits and phrases

as she empties the recycling. We speak
  a language hodgepodge. Afterwards,

I can't remember what was said in which:
  my Spanish, once survival-level, now dusty

and heavily reliant on grace; her English
  better, but not much. We smile a lot.

A smile carries further than you think.
  I recognize her silhouette across the floor,

her dark hair tied neat, ear buds in place
  as she steers her trashcan down the rows of desks,

creating for everyone a clean slate for the morning.
  As for her name, of course I asked. Twice, I think.

It didn't stick, and now the moment's passed.
  And then today, a chance encounter,

both of us working off-hours, she said she was
  *un poco triste.* Her husband has no *papeles.*

*¿Entiendes?* Her eyes search mine for understanding.
He's been here twenty years, she said, working hard

and now immigration's after him. I barely know
the right questions to ask in any language.

And, oh, her heart is breaking. Her son's heart
is breaking. The lawyer says there's nothing

he can do. I stand with my hand over my heart, wishing
I could fix it but I can't. She speaks. I listen hard.

I understand, not everything, but the important parts.
We hug tight. It's something. It's important.

But, of course, it's not enough.

# How They Met

Let me tell you my pandemic story.
I promise you, it's not the one you think. I mean
way back—the flu that only neutral Spain had the guts
to document during the World War and so
got saddled with its name.
1918, people in their prime falling like stars
and just as quickly.
I don't need to paint that picture, primed
as we have been for tragedy. Except to add
the uniforms. Smart lines, matching hats,
the crease just so. Picture him:
small and trim, enlisted in his best hope
forward from the orphanage.
Picture her, the darling baby of the family,
full grown and persuasive, which is say,
somehow her parents gave her range to volunteer
with the Red Cross. They met in ambulances,
ferrying the sick. I wonder if they thought about the risk.
I wonder where the lines of duty and compassion met,
where purpose and bravado—why does anyone
serve others? Picture an apple shared, a chocolate bar,
a taste of gallows humor. At some point they became
more social and less distanced.

Her parents bemoaned his upbringing. Still, they pulled it off.
The pandemic found its end (after so many others' endings) and
they lived. They carved a life together.
They produced my grandfather. Think of all the kindnesses
that pave our paths, yours, and mine.
The words of comfort murmured to the sick,
the ambulances that arrived, the company within
that made the task of healing
light.

# Midnight Kayaking

How many lights in blackness. Jupiter has set, the Milky Way winds
clear as any road.

Bioluminescence streams out from my bow,
eddies with each paddle dip. I scan
for your brief lighted trail

find you almost close enough to touch.
We are skimming on the surface of a thousand interactions

a lobster trapped, a cormorant
spreads its feathers wide and drying in the dark

a supernova ruptures millions of years off and yes
I have always been afraid of sharks and
sudden accidents.

I would not have come tonight except
you shouldered your kayak down the beach and paused
at the silent edge of water.

Down the bay, the seals roiled, grumbling like stomachs.
I keep having to remember

how much is alive. How we are alive inside it. I paddle to you and we sit

night-blinded, kayaks linked
while the ocean carries us like driftwood down the bay.

# First Anniversary

Our first wedding anniversary
was sunnier than Our Big Day and hot.
We slept in, ate cinnamon rolls

for lunch. Did four loads of laundry.
Tried to make the place the way it ought
to look between repeated calls

to say congrats! A year already!
The delphiniums you bought
in wedding colors, blues and purples,

shed quickly. You biked to the library
to finish up some grading. Not
because you wanted to. I culled

strawberries for pie, treasuring
how this morning, I'd made you spot
the answer to a dozen clues, recall

that first dress that wowed (you checked every
one) before you got your card and chocolate.
We made love, our gestures awed and gentle

as the first time. I know I rarely
write you poems, lacking words, and caught
by other pressing matters. You settle

me. We've steadied in. On this first yearly
day of us, you're the wearer of my thoughts.
Our kitchen floor is strewn with petals.

# Biking to Work, Three Days into Fall

Suddenly, the stretch of trail smells like English muffins:
rubbery ones we mashed at camp with too much peanut butter,
gummed and swallowed, still waking up, stalling because
what came next involved a literal plunge. "It's not cold,"
the counselors gritted, avenging their own teen-hoods
from the dock. I was twelve, slip-straight. My bathing suit
bagged sadly at the butt. I hated it, jumped in to hide it
while the lake seized all my skin and shrank it down to
bones and squeals and peanut butter. Here's what grips me:
I was happy. This is not nostalgia speaking.
I feared drowning and stuck-lockers. Worry split my hair.
The harsh teen world was hovering, and yet, and yet. Happy
bobbing in the water. Happy chattering, then sun.

What a work we've done on "happy:" hyped it up
like ecstasy, expected it so long, suspicious when it comes
that it is only here to leave us. Doesn't "happy" always end
the story? Won't it leave us plastic smiles and yawning cherubs
with their harps, while in our books and films the many shades
of suffering garner critical praise? Enough—

this is not a ranting day. The bike trail meets the road, all
gas-and-leaves, two miles to go. Deadline waiting, and I'm proud.
My legs propel me; thoughts scan backward to the lake I loved
full-heartedly, the way I love so many things. It lapped us, soft,
to sleep each night. It held morning mist gentle as a cupped palm,
and when the day bloomed, let it rise.

# Endless

That summer, we tent our way across the West,
give ourselves in awe to vast Montana.
The space and speed of highway! My first encounter
with one stark line of road on the horizon: block it
with your hand, and what remains is green and sky
in perfect halves.

It is the summer before children, when the daylight
stretches wide as future. We make plans as we go,
thinking only of our needs and wonders.
This, before GPS made every road seem knowable.

Long weeks we linger at Glacier, where,
even in July we pull wool hats down low to sleep,
wake listening as the day tunes its symphony.
You coax the night's embers into blaze for coffee.
There, one morning, striding down a path,
we give right-of-way to an enormous moose.
Scrambling into forest, we pant behind a log and gape
as Mama Moose and baby canter past, all knobby knees
and incongruous grace.

I pocket that moment in my mind,
tucked next to that night-storm, where lightning
cracked the eggshell of the sky
but never broke it open. I made you huddle
with me in the stuffy car: safe, I said, from metal
tent poles, while mosquitoes amassed
like zombie hordes at every window, ready.

It was long minutes before you could convince me
that the storm was endless miles off.

My perspective shatters and reforms.
We are inconsequential to the sky but everything
to one another, charting our casual way
that summer before children.

We dip our hands in the Pacific, then,
suddenly road-weary, drive 24-plus hours straight,
eastward toward home, as the summer sun
continues to rise and rise.

# Autumn Ghazal: Wisconsin

Long, low buildings nestled into fields. Startled pockets of trees.
Here everything not grown for food huddles for protection.

You murmur when I kiss you, turn your head in sleeping reflex.
I long to slip back deep into the covers and the warmth of you.

Darkness when I rise for work, mist pooling on the long, low roads.
Clumped and muddy fields, as though somebody has broken them.

The radio hums with politics, with who's attacking who, and what
each candidate will do to change us. We have lost so much, they tell us.

We debated politics last night over dry red wine. You suspect false
promises. My fingers whispered on your skin: hope, perhaps a child.

Sun slow to rise. Stalks clattering, all that remains after the harvest.
Autumn holds more shifting than true change. You nuzzle, slumber on.

# The Woman on the Road

We do not speak, the afternoon I pass the woman
on the red dirt road, carrying her daughter on her back.
The girl, convulsed with fever, beneath the mountains,
hazed with heat. Her feet thump the woman's knees,
her arms encircle the woman's throat. She walks
because the road goes on and on.
        And now, tonight,
I am a thousand miles away, and still she's plodding
through my thoughts, toward hope of health and
promises. I do not know if they arrived. I had no car
to offer. Tomorrow will be full of small but
consequential things, to me. Dear Father, if a prayer
can cover past as well as future, be the driver on the road
who stops to take them in. Be the woman's shoes.
Be the grip of her girl's fingers, linked to hold and hold.

*Northern Togo*

# Nesting

We have nestled deep in winter, welcomed quiet to our home
while quiet remains possible. Our embraces, tender, as our child
swells by ounces in the space between our hearts. Everything
that's rich and sweet I place inside my mouth, wishing milk
and honey for her in the years to come. We bed early, wake
to gray. Light the Christmas lights against the darkening at 2 p.m.
Thick flakes swirl outside but never seem to land. Human birth
and Holy season, taking their sweet time, and we have all our lives
to come to know who will be born. It is enough, for now,
to call friends without visiting. To watch the neighbor boy score
another hockey goal in his garage. He fakes and dodges, heads in early.
I wish him scores of cousins and a field for play. Soon, thaw and water
breaking. But not yet, not yet. Snow-globe sky around us. Swelling
amniotic nest. It is enough to love across the distances, for now.

# When People Know You Are a Poet

It can happen anywhere.
Friends or neighbors telling you the news and weather
segue into a tale whose end your arms anticipate
like a box of weights: "You should write a poem about this."
They grin in expectation.

Say it's Sunday,
and the altar candles have been struggling all sermon
(one extinguished, the other threatening to snuff
the symbolic presence of God) until an altar boy, pressed
into action by a nervous deacon, scurries up at Offering
with the lighter. Afterwards, you're standing with your coffee
and your pleasant greetings when they circle, hope-eyed.

"It's a poem about duty,"
says the deacon. "Who's been slacking off behind the scenes,
forgetting to trim the wicks?" It's not an accusation from his lips,
but eager mystery. He knows everything important happens
behind-the-scenes. Someone skips the benediction weekly
to make coffee. Someone sharpens pencils in the pews
so we can scribble prayers on strips of bulletin, find them
folded in our pants on laundry day, and pray.

"I don't know how it would go,"
says a woman, small and gray, whose name you nearly
remember. "It would say something about love, and how
difficult it sometimes is, and the poem would end
with a little boy rushing to bring light."

Do not tell them no.
Do not joke that it takes more than a Word in the Beginning,
nor speak to them of yesterday's fiasco, when you drank
too much coffee and could do nothing to improve a blank screen.
Nod your head. Agree that they have spotted something
tremulous and rich, tucked within the everyday.
They did not have to tell you this. Thank them for the gift.

# Palm Sunday in the North

Every Easter, Grandma bought us hats and lace gloves
with itchy seams stitched thick along each finger.
We wore them only once a year, just one hour, to church.
A perfect 1950s picture, a generation once-removed:
hats with ribbons, hair in curls, floral pastel dresses.

Every year, Easter dawned too cold to wear them.
Every year, despite the past, we somehow felt betrayed.
We begged to go with puffed-sleeves bared and shivering,
but no: we donned white bulky cardigans, no friend to
any dress. Mollified with jelly beans snuck into play purses,
we chewed color by color, made them stretch through the sermon.

Holy Week begins this year, fittingly resistant. Of course
the sky is woolen-bright, the trees self-protective. April snow cascades
in chunky flakes, slantwise. Spring snow—an unfair pairing.
A guarantee of cardigans. I bundle my daughter, take my seat
among adults still slicked from their winter cocoons. We shrug
our coats into the pews, while girls look on with hurry-up eyes.

The snowfall we so eagerly arrange around the manger
shocks us with its lingering at Easter. We sing hymns with
outward reservation, hoard chocolate, send cards with empty
crosses. I know, I know that the promise Easter bears is a greater
hope than spring, but we are a northern folk, near-sighted,
long on cold and introspection. Crocuses wouldn't hurt.

# St. Francis in the Garden

What interests me is not the bird
alighted on his outstretched hand,
but how he leans as if to break, himself,
into flight. This statue of St Francis,
balanced on his toes, precarious
as Barbie. The lamb clutched beneath
his arm should ground him, weigh him down,
but his cloak falls, wing-like, over it.
Bronzed eyes gazing skyward
as though saying to the creatures
he so often told of God, lead on
and I will follow. No word of physics,
no internal editor clucking doubts. No,
this is faith defying gravity.
In this moment before footfall,
everything is possible.

# Inspiration Arrives Half-Wild

but only half.
(Don't let them tell you otherwise.)

Which is to say, it's possible to strike a deal, if you ask it nicely,
to come calling at a more sensible time. Lunch break, say,
or naptime. So long as you lure it with the gift that everything else
wants too:

Your Complete Attention.

Which is to say, don't waste that appointed hour on something sensible
like lunch.
I can tell you, there are days I watch my daughter's heavy lids shutter
with such wriggling anticipation, already hooked by a line—

I can tell you, too, how I've failed to show and lost

the scent

up to a year.

It's a case of mutual tracking, you see.
We both of us have been elusive, inspiration and I. Or, as people
often put it

busy…

Which is why O'Hara's lunchtime poems make sense to me now:
all those breathless poems / rolling thoughts / bleeding
into others half-formed

Who has time for punctuation?

He'd made a date with inspiration. Kept his end up. Marked the clock.
Can't you see him opening his notebook, calling
"Alright, boys!"
(You know he would've called them 'boys'.)
"Now's your chance. Let's give it all you've got."

# Embedded

I want you to imagine
living somewhere else.

Look around, and listen.
Find the rhythm of the everyday
that locals have stopped
noticing long ago.

Now you must go discover
where to buy your bread and oil.
You must learn anew how to greet
and give and offer thanks,
bumbling to show yourself
through this new language, words
cracked and drifting like icebergs.

Does it thrill you?
Does it make you want to sprint,
clicking your heels down the unknown street,
to photograph and jot notes
and shake strangers by the hand?

I used to be this way. I dreamed
of embedding myself in each new landscape.
I sought to soak cultures through my pores
until I became myself and something new
at the same time.

I collected continents.

I wonder where she went, this wanderer.
Is she coiled, purring, wedged
inside me, waiting? And for what?

Ask me to imagine life in a new land
and before the blush of inspiration pales,
I'm caught up in the grind
of moving, selling, finding
a new dentist. Not to mention
the myriad goodbyes. Blame parenthood,
perhaps, but it's exhausting,
the sheer thought of sheering roots
I planted, coaxed for years to grow.

Today, I walk the same routes
as last year and the year before. I greet
neighbors, ask after the pharmacist's
young son.

I don't know what to tell her,
this dear girl I used to be, except,
I hope she isn't disappointed.
She knows I've always wanted to belong.

# What is Revealed, What is Washed Away

When I wake, we are surrounded.
All the sea beyond this point of land
whitewashed by the fog.

Even the hum of lobster boats,
the conversations of the gulls
have been reverently tamped down.

I am not an early riser, but the cold
shook me from my quilts,
demanded attention.

The ocean breathes and cozies into shoals.
A groan which could be seal or dock,
the clap of wings against the water.

Yesterday, the tide delivered hundreds of dead fish.
They pockmarked the bay, white-bellied, reeking:
bait fish whose oil once burned bright as whales',

whose planted flesh helped corn and squash to grow.
Castoffs from a careless trawler.
It took hours for the gulls to find them.

We dipped kayak paddles past the wreckage.
Each fish, long as my forearm. They floated,
even ripped in two. Even with their feathered bones exposed.

This early morning, across the bay, the tips of evergreens
declare themselves. The fog thins quickly after that.
Boats emerge. The docks. The birds,

taking flight. Their wings applaud against the surface.
Their volume rises toward the day.
And on the surface of the water:
not a single fish.

*Pemaquid, Maine*

# Pause

It's been too long since you have wandered like a poet in a forest,
not
rushing
anywhere.
Leading with your ears and eyes.

You know the sound of a forest, don't you? You must—
how the rich green growing feeds you, opens
all that's closed and clenched. You know, I hope, how it is
to stop near a pond where the frog-song is loudest and
let the forest breathe. Inhale its offering. Give it back.

You know, then, that you cannot stay forever. The onslaught
of mosquitoes, your own hunger
will move you on before long. You know how it is
to emerge cleansed by green, straighter now, re-centered.
How long it takes before the world resumes its former pace—

that is entirely up to you.

# For My Husband

I wanted to curl against his hot morning
skin and breathe without clocks ticking
I wanted to declare today a celebration
in his honor and cook him omelets studded
with cheddar and whimsy I wanted him to
do the dishes he said he'd do last night I wanted
to chasten motivate stroke encourage cry Get out
of bed! cry Yes you can sleep in take the day
while I without guile or selfishness mind
the child we both love I wanted to haul
the soggy burden of depression from his
chest and free him I wanted to heave my
frustration like a wet spreading blanket
over him and demand he fix it all I wanted
to call him at work and tell him I loved him
tell him my love for him is a fact of life
immutable tell him now once more in case
he forgot from this morning when he
stumbled over Duplos in the still-dark
to get dressed tell him in case his car slipped
skidded from the road upended on the short
drive home to me

*after Grace Paley*

# Weeding

The day I learned my father's cancer
was not gone, that it could,
in the doctor's words,
"pop back up again,"
I stalked out to the garden
and began pulling weeds.
They multiplied beneath
my noticing, vibrant stems and
guts of grass that snapped defiantly
at base. I dug in. I knew, even
as I tugged out long pale fangs of root
that I was trying to heal by metaphor.
I knew it would not work.
I couldn't bear to leave a shred
to re-grow and re-route
our lives. I hurled the waste
into the woods, wishing for fire.
How could I expect to be relieved?
I left the earth opened:
great dark clumps of mulch upturned
everywhere my hands had touched.

# Terra Firma

May again. At last, the snow melts to reveal
the darkened patch of earth where, last fall, I planted
garlic with my daughter. I showed her how to dig,
swaddled the dark patch with hay, let winter bury all.
Now I long to see the first green shoots—proof,
should they arrive, that it's possible to survive
our coldest winter yet. I watch, I keen, I sing for them
to grow green and tall and thick spice-rooted.
In this way, I'm like the ancients, hovering near
the first curling stalks of spring, waiting the long
wait for what the soil eventually gives. In this way,
I'm like the ancient Hebrews, who relied on soil,
who carried it from their homes when they traveled;
a sprinkling of dirt could turn desert into holy land.
This, when the world was measured in footsteps,
intimated from the stars, when dragons lurked
at the edge of our maps—they lurk, still, though now
they go by other names, though now our maps grow
ever wider and more detailed. In this way,
I'm like the scholars: able to diagram, by rote,
the earth down to its molten core. The earth's core,
yes, but not four inches below the soil, where blind
white bulbs of garlic might or might not be readying
to birth themselves into the air. To peek now
would undo everything. There is a multitude of
information ready at a keystroke; there are pictures
of distant nebulae and the inner workings of
viruses. And in spite of everything, perhaps
because of it, lies the long wait for spring. In this way,
let me be like the generations, hoping to be sustained,
trusting the ground to keep its eternal secrets.

# Holy Ground

On our evening walk, we confront
a tree in perfect yellow bloom, releasing
its leaves one by one, spinning to the earth.

What kind of being would not pause
to watch such stunning and
deliberate undress?

How every leaf somehow knows the precise
moment to let go. Yellow by yellow, they fall.
There is no wind, only the tree's decision.

And they do not go silently. They clatter
on the pine below and land upon the earth
like rain, but more slowly.

# The Aunt in the Attic

Toward the end, she wrapped everything in brown paper and string:
the china doll, the silverware,

each day's *County Crier*. Stacked them in her attic according to a system
of her own invention.

The attic stairs were steep. She climbed one-handed, lugging parcels.
I picture her content.

Was it preservation? an unburdening? (My grandmother, her only niece,
simply will not speculate.

Aunts like her were suffered-through. Un-spoken-of. Better a mad woman
in the attic than out in the streets.)

The stripping-down came later. First the hat and matching gloves,
wrapped and bound, unnecessary.

Then the shirt, the sensible skirt, her bra and panties (unmatched).
She called down cheerful-naked

to the paper boy—her words polite, her erect piano-teacher posture,
her old breasts dangling.

I do not know how long it was before she died. Small towns can be
possessive—she was never "put away."

Imagine the rediscovery upon her death, my grandmother's grim
excavation. Here, a stack of twenties. Here,

oatmeal petrified in its yellow bowl. Dressed, they all look similar.
All those years, my great-great-aunt,

who had no children, listened with prim correctness to decades of
belabored scales. She demonstrated Mozart

to students who would listen, never hinting what she carried—what
she passed, almost directly, down to me.

# Loved

They arrived the same day: birth notice and obituary.
Best friend's newborn daughter [click] then suddenly
Aunt Happy's face as I had never seen it, 1940s-beautiful
with perfect curls; date for her memorial, condolences
to the church.

Happy, who when she wed Dick Bright had such a name.
He fought in WWII; she taught until the children came.
That was all I knew. When we met, she was old already.
(So my friend will seem to her new baby, a fixed factor
in the world.)

Imagine Uncle Dick after 50 years, trying to condense
everything he loved about his wife to sentences.
I wonder if those words were how he held her, near the end,
when something in her brain misplaced her family
like keys.

I want the memories of her I never had—because she lived,
because in her photo she is smiling in a perfect light, and maybe
after posing she made some clever comment. I want to capture
every moment, anchor it for safe keeping. But life, like love,
resists such grasping.

Even my dear friend, joyous and exhausted, set down
the camera when her baby cried for milk.
Let me circle back again, then, to newborn daughters.
The future's glowing and unknowable. See how
with such fierce abandon we are loved and loved
and loved.

# Acknowledgements

I am grateful to the editors of the following publications in which some of these poems first appeared:

"Midnight Kayaking" has appeared in *Other Voice International*, *Ocean Magazine*, and *Broad Wings, Long Legs: a Rookery of Heron Poems* (North Star Press, April 2024)

"Dartmouth Scientists Discover High Levels of Arsenic in Rice" was published in *Colliers Online*

Emily Bright is a weekend host for MPR News, where she also covers arts and books. She holds an MFA in poetry from the University of Minnesota and a BA from Williams College. She is the author of a chapbook, *Glances Back*, and co-author of *Powerful Ideas in Teaching: Creating Environments Where Students Want to Learn*. She lives in the Twin Cities with her family.